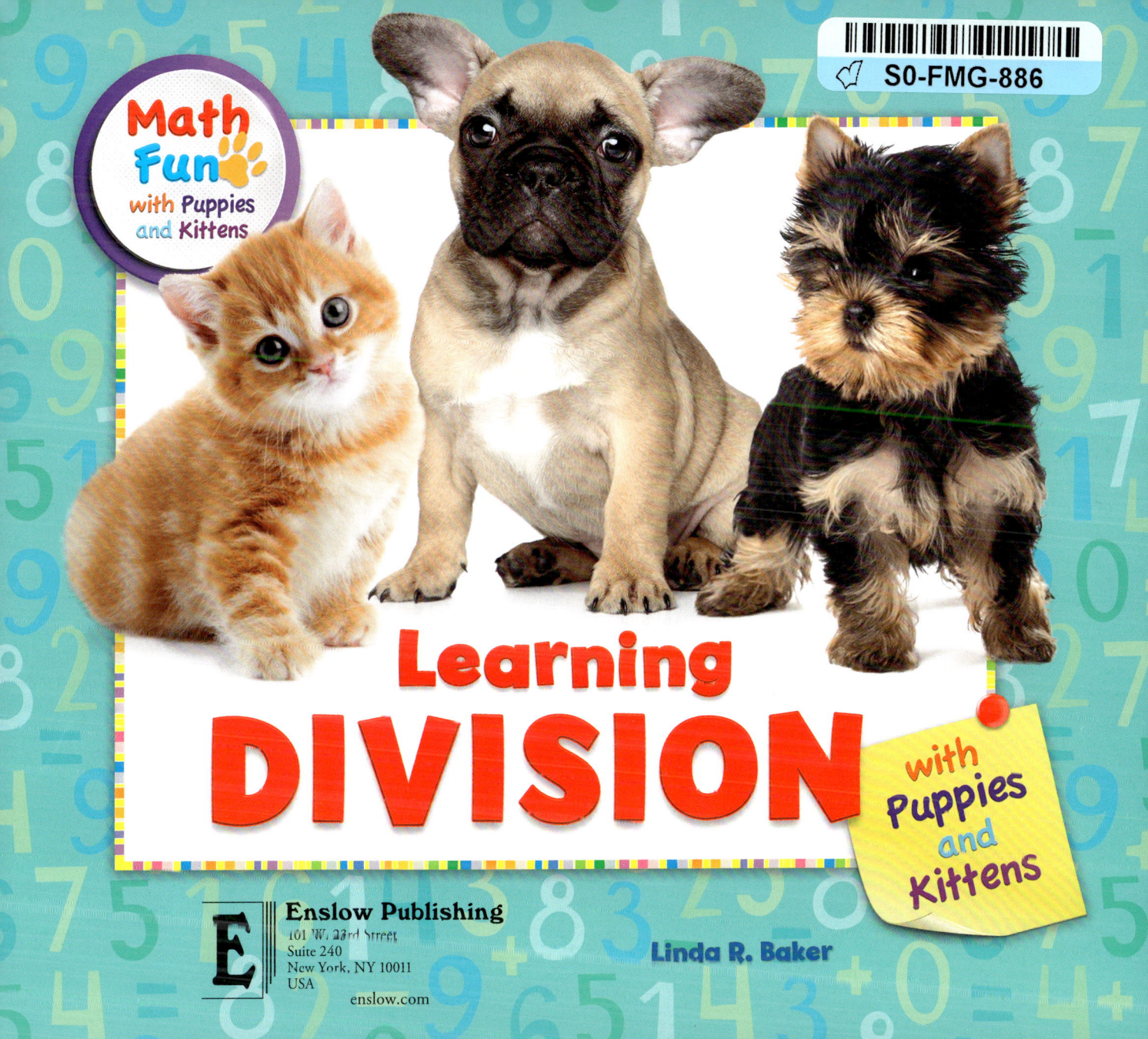

Words to Know

basic Simplest.

divide To sort a given number of objects into equal groups.

dividend The number that is divided into groups of equal size.

divisor The number of groups the dividend will be divided into.

equal Of the same value.

operation A way to get one number using other numbers by following special rules.

quotient The answer to a division problem.

value The amount or worth of something.

Contents

Words to Know 2
Division 4
Division Rules 6
Learn to Divide by 1 8
Learn to Divide by 2 10
Learn to Divide by 3 12
Learn to Divide by 4 14
Learn to Divide by 5 16
Learn to Divide by 6 18
Learn to Divide by 7 20
Learn to Divide by 8 22
Learn to Divide by 9 24
Learn to Divide by 10 26
Review Division Facts 28
Activities with Division 30
Learn More 31
Index 32

Division

Division is the kind of math you use to share, or take apart, a number of objects into two or more **equal** groups or parts.

The **quotient** tells you how many of the objects will be in each group. You can count puppies and kittens to learn how division works!

6 ÷ 2 is a division fact.

Division facts can be written in four ways:

$$6 \div 2 = 3$$

$$6 / 2 = 3$$

$$2 \overline{)6} \text{with quotient } 3$$

$$\frac{6}{2} = 3$$

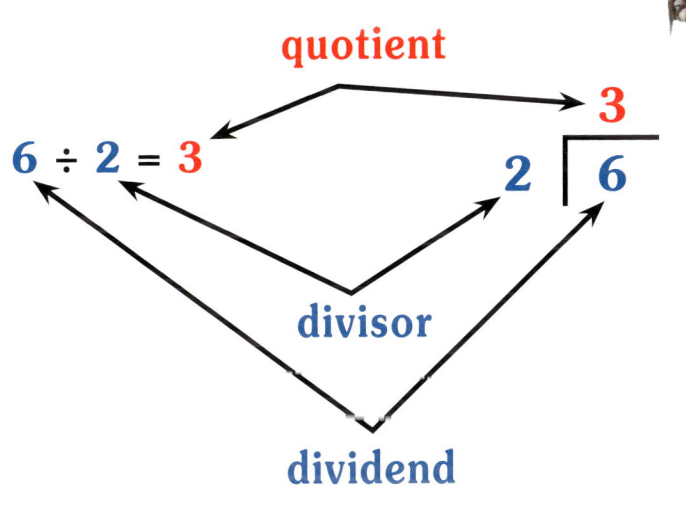

Four Math Operations

Division is one of the four basic operations used in math. The other three are addition, subtraction, and multiplication.

There are five parts to a division fact:

(1) The **dividend** is the number that is **divided** into groups of equal size: **6**.

(2) The division sign (÷) means divide.

(3) The **divisor** is the number of groups the dividend will be divided into: **2**.

(4) The equal sign (=) tells you to solve the problem.

(5) The quotient, or answer, comes after the equal sign or above the division box: **3**.

Division Rules

- No number can be divided by **0**; the divisor can never be **0**.

- Zero (**0**) can be divided by any number (the divisor) and the quotient will always be **0**. Zero has no **value**. If you divide **0** into any number of parts, there will always be **0** in each part.

- If you divide any number by **1** the quotient will always be that number. For example, look at **5 ÷ 1 = 5**. If you divide **5** into **1** part, it will contain all **5** items.

- The order of divisor and dividend cannot be changed without changing the quotient.

- Dividing can be thought of as repeated subtraction until you get to **0**. For example, **6** puppies have **2** beds. How many puppies in each bed? Start by putting **1** puppy in each of the **2** beds; you have **4** puppies left: **6 − 2 = 4**.

If you put **1** of the **4** puppies in each of the **2** beds, you then have **2** puppies left: **4 − 2 = 2**.

Finally, put **1** of each of the last **2** puppies in each bed: **2 − 2 = 0**.

Three subtractions get you the same answer you would get with division. There will be **3** puppies in each bed, or **2** groups of **3**.

🐾 Division can be checked by multiplying the quotient times the divisor or the divisor times the quotient. Unlike division, the order of factors in multiplication can be changed.

Learn to Divide by 1

Remember, when you divide by **1**, the quotient is always the same as the dividend. Try it!

Four (**4**) puppies are playing in **1** yard. How many puppies are playing in the yard?

4 ÷ 1

There is only **1** group and it contains all **4** of the puppies.

1 ÷ 1 = 1	6 ÷ 1 = 6
2 ÷ 1 = 2	7 ÷ 1 = 7
3 ÷ 1 = 3	8 ÷ 1 = 8
4 ÷ 1 = 4	9 ÷ 1 = 9
5 ÷ 1 = 5	10 ÷ 1 = 10

Learn to Divide by 2

Eight (8) kittens are playing with 2 balls of yarn. If the same number of kittens are playing with each ball of yarn, how many kittens will be playing with each ball of yarn?

8 ÷ 2

There are **4** kittens playing with each ball of yarn.

Some numbers cannot be divided evenly by **2**. Do you see which ones? The odd numbers (**1**, **3**, **5**, **7**, **9**) cannot be divided evenly by **2**.

$2 \div 2 = 1$
$4 \div 2 = 2$
$6 \div 2 = 3$
$8 \div 2 = 4$
$10 \div 2 = 5$
$12 \div 2 = 6$
$14 \div 2 = 7$
$16 \div 2 = 8$
$18 \div 2 = 9$
$20 \div 2 = 10$

= 4

Number Family

Multiplication facts can be used to figure out division problems. Division and multiplication are the opposite of each other and can help you learn the basic facts. For example:

$2 \times 4 = 8$
$4 \times 2 = 8$
$8 \div 2 = 4$
$8 \div 4 = 2$

This is called a number family.

Learn to Divide by 3

Nine (9) puppies have 3 beds to cuddle up in. How many puppies will cuddle up in each bed for a nap?

9 ÷ 3

There will be **3** puppies cuddled up in each bed.

Notice that the dividends are counting up by **3** and the quotients are counting up by **1**. Try this by dividing objects such as beads, cubes, or counters into groups of **3**. Notice that some numbers cannot be evenly divided by **3**.

$3 \div 3 = 1$
$6 \div 3 = 2$
$9 \div 3 = 3$
$12 \div 3 = 4$
$15 \div 3 = 5$
$18 \div 3 = 6$
$21 \div 3 = 7$
$24 \div 3 = 8$
$27 \div 3 = 9$
$30 \div 3 = 10$

= 3

Learn to Divide by 4

There are **20** kittens in Aunt Martha's house, and only **4** large bowls of cat food. How many kittens can gather evenly at each bowl?

20 ÷ 4

Five (5) kittens can gather at each bowl.

Try this with beads or counters again. Notice that each dividend increases by **4** and not every number can be evenly divided by **4**. It is like counting by 4s.

4 ÷ 4 = 1	24 ÷ 4 = 6
8 ÷ 4 = 2	28 ÷ 4 = 7
12 ÷ 4 = 3	32 ÷ 4 = 8
16 ÷ 4 = 4	36 ÷ 4 = 9
20 ÷ 4 = 5	40 ÷ 4 = 10

= 5

Learn to Divide by 5

Ten (10) puppies have 5 toys to play with. How many puppies will have to share each dog toy if they share them evenly?

10 ÷ 5

Two (**2**) puppies will have to share each dog toy. Counting by 5s will help you with these division facts. Notice the dividends are **5**, **10**, **15**, **20** and so on.

$5 \div 5 = 1$
$10 \div 5 = 2$
$15 \div 5 = 3$
$20 \div 5 = 4$
$25 \div 5 = 5$
$30 \div 5 = 6$
$35 \div 5 = 7$
$40 \div 5 = 8$
$45 \div 5 = 9$
$50 \div 5 = 10$

 = **2**

High Five!
Any number ending in **5** or **0**, no matter how big or small, can be divided by **5**.

Learn to Divide by 6

Eighteen (**18**) kittens lie in the sunlight coming in through **6** windows. How many kittens can lie in the sunlight by each window if they share evenly?

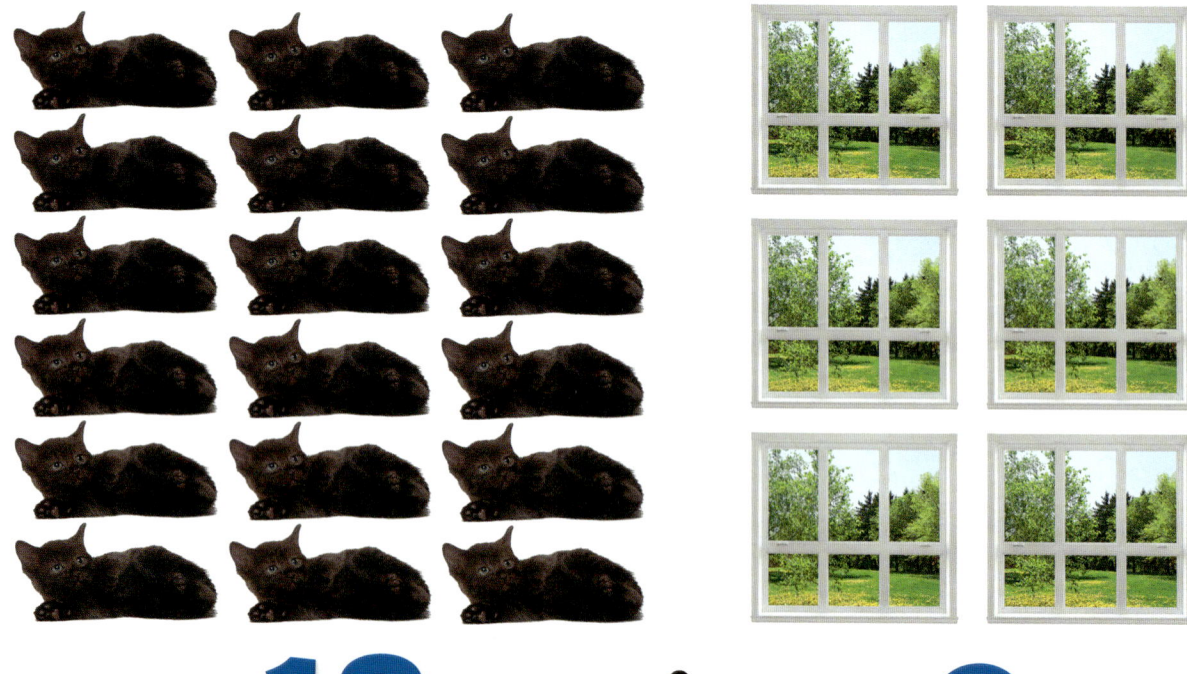

18 ÷ 6

Three (**3**) kittens can share the sunlight from each window.

6 ÷ 6 =	1	36 ÷ 6 =	6
12 ÷ 6 =	2	42 ÷ 6 =	7
18 ÷ 6 =	**3**	48 ÷ 6 =	8
24 ÷ 6 =	4	54 ÷ 6 =	9
30 ÷ 6 =	5	60 ÷ 6 =	10

Learn to Divide by 7

Fourteen (**14**) puppies were in the dog park. If there were **7** people in the park with the puppies and they each had the same number of puppies with them, how many puppies did each person have?

14 ÷ 7

Each person had **2** puppies at the dog park.

7 ÷ 7 = 1	42 ÷ 7 = 6
14 ÷ 7 = 2	49 ÷ 7 = 7
21 ÷ 7 = 3	56 ÷ 7 = 8
28 ÷ 7 = 4	63 ÷ 7 = 9
35 ÷ 7 = 5	70 ÷ 7 = 10

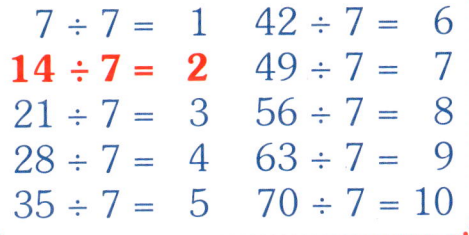

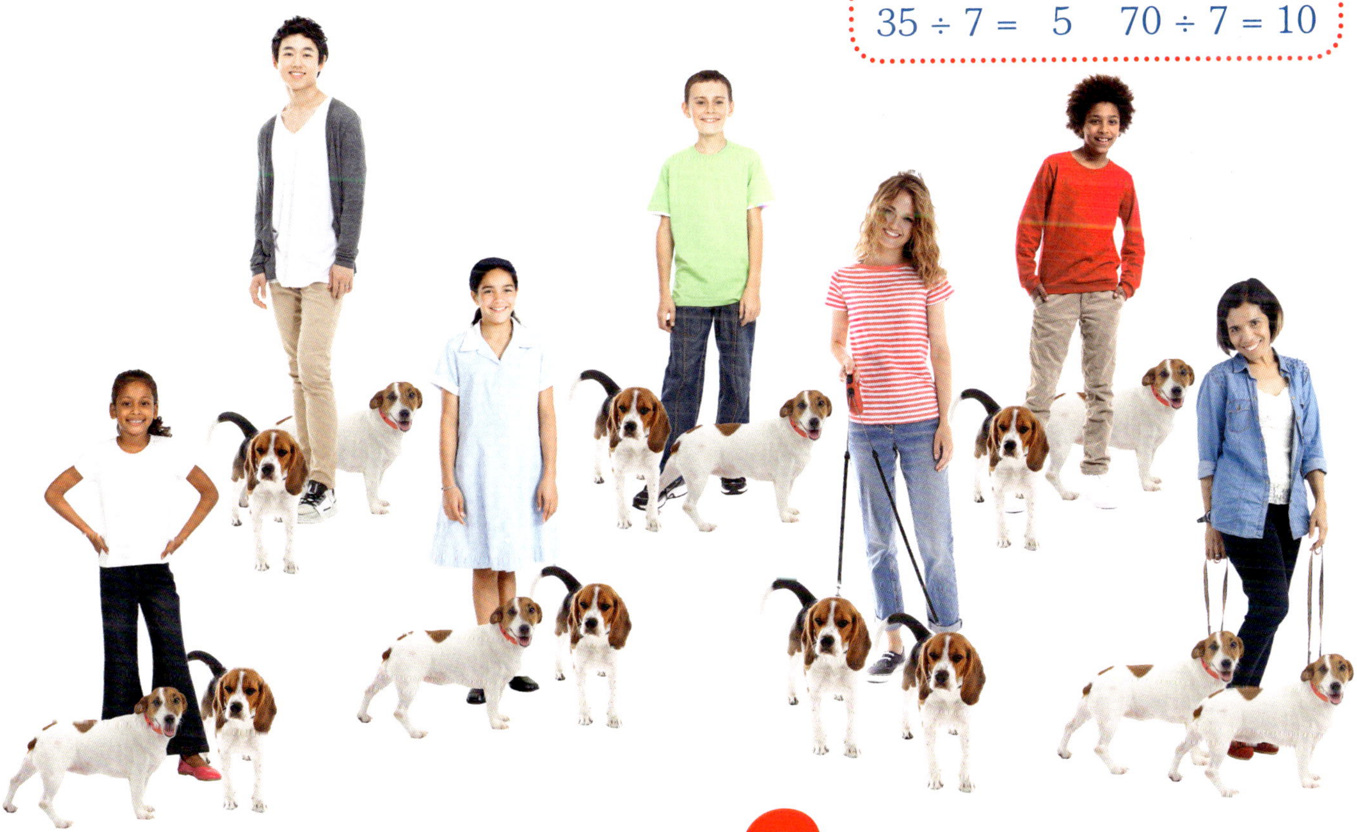

= 2

Learn to Divide by 8

There are **16** puppies and kittens on the farm. There are **8** people looking to adopt the same number of animals. How many animals will each person go home with?

16 **8**

Using Addition to Understand Division

Notice when you divide by any given number that the next dividend will be that number higher than the last dividend. For example, look at $8 \div 8 = 1$. To keep dividing evenly we must add $8 + 8 = 16$, and 16 will be our next dividend: $16 \div 8 = 2$. Look at the fact table. Every new dividend is 8 more than the one before it. This is true for all the division problems we have explored so far. Also notice that the quotient goes up by one with each math fact.

Each person will go home with **2** animals.

$8 \div 8 = 1$
$16 \div 8 = 2$
$24 \div 8 = 3$
$32 \div 8 = 4$
$40 \div 8 = 5$
$48 \div 8 = 6$
$56 \div 8 = 7$
$64 \div 8 = 8$
$72 \div 8 = 9$
$80 \div 8 = 10$

= 2

Learn to Divide by 9

There are a lot of kittens at the animal shelter, **45** in all. If we let the kittens out in even groups to play on **9** cat trees, how many kittens will play on each cat tree?

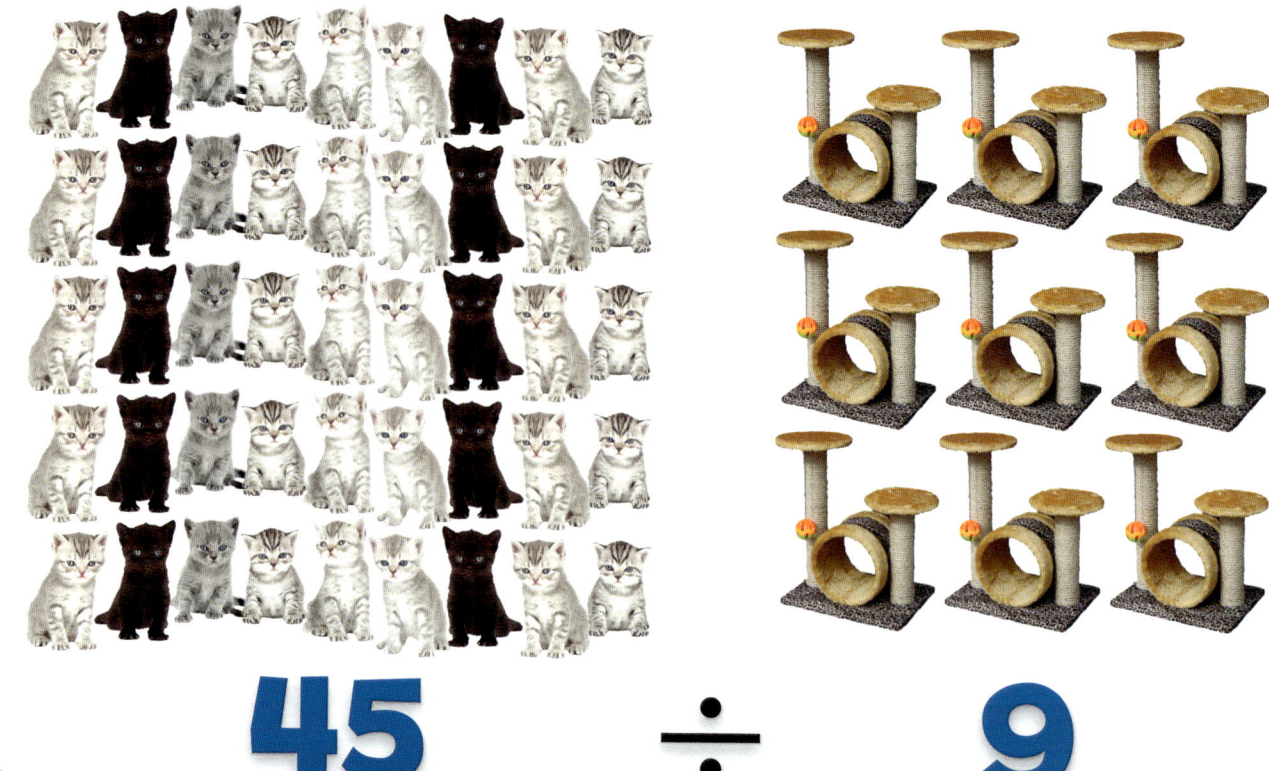

45 ÷ 9

Nifty Nines

There is something very special about the 9s. Can you spot it? The two digits in every dividend of 9 add up to 9: 1 + 8 = 9, 2 + 7 = 9, 3 + 6 = 9, 4 + 5 = 9. This will help you with your multiplication facts as well.

$9 \div 9 = 1$
$18 \div 9 = 2$
$27 \div 9 = 3$
$36 \div 9 = 4$
$45 \div 9 = 5$
$54 \div 9 = 6$
$63 \div 9 = 7$
$72 \div 9 = 8$
$81 \div 9 = 9$
$90 \div 9 = 10$

Five (5) kittens will play on each cat tree.

= 5

Learn to Divide by 10

There are **30** puppies entered into obedience school. There are **10** dog trainers. How many puppies are taught by each trainer?

30 10

There are **3** puppies taught by each trainer.

= 3

10 ÷ 10 =	1
20 ÷ 10 =	2
30 ÷ 10 =	**3**
40 ÷ 10 =	4
50 ÷ 10 =	5
60 ÷ 10 =	6
70 ÷ 10 =	7
80 ÷ 10 =	8
90 ÷ 10 =	9
100 ÷ 10 =	10

Division Tip for Tens

Do you see a pattern here? What is it? Every dividend is the same as the quotient with a 0 at the end! Dividing by 10 is very easy!

Review Division Facts

Do you know all the division facts in this book? Take a look!

÷ 1	÷ 2	÷ 3	÷ 4	÷ 5
1 ÷ 1 = 1	2 ÷ 2 = 1	3 ÷ 3 = 1	4 ÷ 4 = 1	5 ÷ 5 = 1
2 ÷ 1 = 2	4 ÷ 2 = 2	6 ÷ 3 = 2	8 ÷ 4 = 2	10 ÷ 5 = 2
3 ÷ 1 = 3	6 ÷ 2 = 3	9 ÷ 3 = 3	12 ÷ 4 = 3	15 ÷ 5 = 3
4 ÷ 1 = 4	8 ÷ 2 = 4	12 ÷ 3 = 4	16 ÷ 4 = 4	20 ÷ 5 = 4
5 ÷ 1 = 5	10 ÷ 2 = 5	15 ÷ 3 = 5	20 ÷ 4 = 5	25 ÷ 5 = 5
6 ÷ 1 = 6	12 ÷ 2 = 6	18 ÷ 3 = 6	24 ÷ 4 = 6	30 ÷ 5 = 6
7 ÷ 1 = 7	14 ÷ 2 = 7	21 ÷ 3 = 7	28 ÷ 4 = 7	35 ÷ 5 = 7
8 ÷ 1 = 8	16 ÷ 2 = 8	24 ÷ 3 = 8	32 ÷ 4 = 8	40 ÷ 5 = 8
9 ÷ 1 = 9	18 ÷ 2 = 9	27 ÷ 3 = 9	36 ÷ 4 = 9	45 ÷ 5 = 9
10 ÷ 1 = 10	20 ÷ 2 = 10	30 ÷ 3 = 10	40 ÷ 4 = 10	50 ÷ 5 = 10

÷ 6	÷ 7	÷ 8	÷ 9	÷ 10
6 ÷ 6 = 1	7 ÷ 7 = 1	8 ÷ 8 = 1	9 ÷ 9 = 1	10 ÷ 10 = 1
12 ÷ 6 = 2	14 ÷ 7 = 2	16 ÷ 8 = 2	18 ÷ 9 = 2	20 ÷ 10 = 2
18 ÷ 6 = 3	21 ÷ 7 = 3	24 ÷ 8 = 3	27 ÷ 9 = 3	30 ÷ 10 = 3
24 ÷ 6 = 4	28 ÷ 7 = 4	32 ÷ 8 = 4	36 ÷ 9 = 4	40 ÷ 10 = 4
30 ÷ 6 = 5	35 ÷ 7 = 5	40 ÷ 8 = 5	45 ÷ 9 = 5	50 ÷ 10 = 5
36 ÷ 6 = 6	42 ÷ 7 = 6	48 ÷ 8 = 6	54 ÷ 9 = 6	60 ÷ 10 = 6
42 ÷ 6 = 7	49 ÷ 7 = 7	56 ÷ 8 = 7	63 ÷ 9 = 7	70 ÷ 10 = 7
48 ÷ 6 = 8	56 ÷ 7 = 8	64 ÷ 8 = 8	72 ÷ 9 = 8	80 ÷ 10 = 8
54 ÷ 6 = 9	63 ÷ 7 = 9	72 ÷ 8 = 9	81 : 9 = 9	90 ÷ 10 = 9
60 ÷ 6 = 10	70 ÷ 7 = 10	80 ÷ 8 = 10	90 ÷ 9 = 10	100 ÷ 10 = 10

Activities with Division

Make Flashcards

Write a division fact on an index card on one side. Write the answer on the other side. Make as many flash cards as you want. Test yourself! How many did you get right?

Look for Patterns

When you are on the lookout for patterns, you will begin to notice things in sets and think about how these sets can be divided into smaller sets. Look at packages of pencils, markers, or crayons. How many different ways can the package be divided evenly?

Keep a Book of Division Families

Now you know that every division problem is a family of numbers that go together and can be used for multiplication, too. Write each number family on a piece of paper. Create a cover out of construction paper. Then, staple the cover and pages together. You can add pictures if you want!

Learn More

Books

Brack, Amanda, and Sky Pony Press. **Math for Minecrafters: Adventures in Multiplication and Division.** New York, NY: Sky Pony Press, 2017.

Midthun, Joseph. **Division**. Chicago, IL: World Book, Inc., 2016.

Thinking Kids. **Brainy Book of Multiplication and Division**. Greensboro, NC: Thinking Kids, 2015.

Williams, Zella, and Rebecca Wingard-Nelson. **Word Problems Using Multiplication and Division**. New York, NY: Enslow Publishing, 2017.

Websites

Arcademics
www.arcademics.com
Play fun division games and other math practice games.

Doctor Genius, Division
www.mathabc.com/math-3rd-grade/division/division
Solve division problems online!

Sheppard Software, Math
www.sheppardsoftware.com/math.htm
Enjoy more interactive division games!

Index

addition, 23
dividend, 5, 13, 23
division facts, 4, 5, 17, 23, 25, 28–29
division rules, 6–7
divisor, 5
factors, 7
multiplication, 7, 11, 25
number family, 11
odd numbers, 11
operations, 5
quotient, 4, 13, 23
subtraction, 6–7

For Fiona and Champ, my two favorite pups
Published in 2018 by Enslow Publishing, LLC.
101 W. 23rd Street, Suite 240, New York, NY 10011
Copyright © 2018 by Enslow Publishing, LLC.
All rights reserved.
No part of this book may be reproduced by any means without the written permission of the publisher.

Library of Congress Cataloging-in-Publication Data
Names: Baker, Linda R., author.
Title: Learning division with puppies and kittens / Linda R. Baker.
Description: New York, NY : Enslow Publishing, 2018. | Series: Math fun with puppies and kittens | Audience: K to grade 3. | Includes bibliographical references and index.
Identifiers: LCCN 2017014574 | ISBN 9780766090880 (library bound) | ISBN 9780766090736 (pbk.) | ISBN 9780766090781 (6 pack)
Subjects: LCSH: Division—Juvenile literature. | Mathematics—Juvenile literature.
Classification: LCC QA115 .B353 2018 | DDC 513.2/14—dc23
LC record available at https://lccn.loc.gov/2017014574

Printed in China

To Our Readers: We have done our best to make sure all websites in this book were active and appropriate when we went to press. However, the author and the publisher have no control over and assume no liability for the material available on those websites or on any websites they may link to. Any comments or suggestions can be sent by email to customerservice@enslow.com.

Photo credits: Cover, p. 1 (kitten) Dmitry Kalinovsky/Shutterstock.com; cover, pp. 1 (puppy, center), 26 (pair of red puppies), 27 (pair of red puppies) Jagodka/Shutterstock.com; cover, p. 1 (puppy, right) Pavel Hlystov/Shutterstock.com; pp. 2 (kitten, left), 22 (puppy and kitten in basket), 23 (puppy and kitten in basket), 26 (yellow puppy), 27 (yellow puppy) Happy monkey/Shutterstock.com; pp. 2 (fluffy puppy), 29 Liliya Kulianionak/Shutterstock.com; p. 2 (last 6 animals from the right) Ermolaev Alexander/Shutterstock.com; p. 4 Oleksandr Lytvynenko/Shutterstock.com; p. 5 Tatiana Katsai/Shutterstock.com; p. 7 (group of puppies, left) ANURAK PONGPATIMET/Shutterstock.com; p. 7 (group of puppies, right) WilleeCole Photography/Shutterstock.com; pp. 8, 9 (puppy) Oksana Kuzmina/Shutterstock.com; pp. 8, 9 (yard) Artazum/Shutterstock.com; pp. 10, 11 (kitten) robert_s/Shutterstock.com; pp. 10, 11 (yarn) Viktor Kunz/Shutterstock.com; pp. 12 (puppy), 13 (puppy), 27 (puppy, bottom) ARTSILENSE/Shutterstock.com; pp. 12, 13 (bed) PH PHOTO STUDIO/Shutterstock.com; pp. 14 (kitten), 15 (kitten), 16 (puppy), 17 (puppy) Nataliya Kuznetsova/Shutterstock.com; pp. 14 (food), 15 (food), 20 (puppy facing front and woman in striped shirt), 21 (puppy facing front and woman in striped shirt) Africa Studio/Shutterstock.com; p. 16 (toys) hd connelly/Shutterstock.com; p. 17 (kitten) Lubava/Shutterstock.com; pp. 18, 19 (kitten) Tony Campbell/Shutterstock.com; pp. 18, 19 (window) GoodMood Photo/Shutterstock.com; pp. 20, 21 (puppy facing sideways and woman in blue shirt) wong sze yuen/Shutterstock.com; pp. 20, 21 (boy in red shirt) Djomas/Shutterstock.com; pp. 20, 21 (man in grey sweater) Hans Kim/Shutterstock.com; pp. 20, 21 (girl in blue dress and girl in white shirt) michaeljung/Shutterstock.com; pp. 20, 21 (boy in green shirt) Catalin Petolea/Shutterstock.com; pp. 22, 23 (group of people) Monkey Business Images/Shutterstock.com; p. 23 (kitten, top left) yevgeniy11/Shutterstock.com; pp. 24, 25 (kittens) bibürcha/Shutterstock.com; pp. 24, 25 (cat tree) Rainy_picasso/Shutterstock.com; p. 25 (puppy) Kalamurzing/Shutterstock.com; pp. 26, 27 (red puppy with head up and woman in yellow shirt) Svetography/Shutterstock.com; pp. 26, 27 (white and gray puppy and woman in purple shirt) Alexey Stiop/Shutterstock.com; pp. 26, 27 (pair of women back-to-back) rnl/Shutterstock.com; pp. 26, 27 (man in blue shirt) mimagephotography/Shutterstock.com; pp. 26, 27 (man with arms up) ESB Professional/Shutterstock.com; pp. 26, 27 (seated group of people) Rido/Shutterstock.com.